Your Brick Oven

Your Brick Oven

Building it and Baking in it

Photographs by Christo Reid

GRUB STREET • LONDON

Published in the 2005 by
Grub Street
4 Rainham Close
London
SW11 6SS
Email: food@grubstreet.co.uk
Web: www.grubstreet.co.uk

First published in Australia by Wakefield Press

Designed by Dean Lahn, Lahn Stafford Design, Adelaide

British Library Cataloguing in Publication Data
A catalogue record for this book is available from the
British Library

ISBN 1 904943 25 X

Printed and bound in Australia by Hyde Park Press,
Adelaide

To my family
past and present

Your Brick Oven

Your brick oven

Strong and true

The fire within burns

Bright for you

For all who walk

The timeless land

You shape your loaves

With sturdy hands

Blessing those who've gone before

You place them on the burning floor

Born of water, earth and air

The bread is made with love and care

By your own sweat you feed your soul

And free God's will to make you whole

Contents

I've long admired Russell Jeavons as one of the most earthy people I know. Who else would have the courage and the confidence to cook as he does, opening his restaurant on only one night of the week so his cooking fits around his own life?

by Maggie Beer

Foreword

Writing down recipes probably goes against the grain for Russell as I suspect he cooks by the seat of his pants with whatever produce he has to hand. But when he starts to write about how to build a brick oven, he's a man on a mission to share all that he's learnt over the years. His practical tips come from a hands-on practitioner who knows how to combine the secrets of a successful oven with the commonsense and experience that I wish Colin and I had had before our many attempts to perfect our brick oven. Even when our final model was finished we were babes in the wood when it came to getting the most out of it. In fact it languished in our yard as nothing but a good idea until we had the good fortune of employing a passionate chef who showed us how to cook in it. This was a process that took place over several great brick-oven-fired nights and gave us the skills we needed to make it truly a part of our life.

In this book Russell starts from scratch with instructions on how to build an oven including all the things missing from ours. From insulating the oven (how I wish we'd known about that!), designing a door that damp rags can be squeezed around to add steam when cooking bread, to tips about tools and locating your oven near a tap to allow for easy cleaning. After reading Russell's book you will have learnt from his mistakes and have all the advantages of his path of continual improvement.

I expect that women will buy this book for their menfolk – lots of women would love a brick oven of their own and, while they might light the initial fire of inspiration in their blokes, once built the oven can quickly become men's business. Firing up the oven is a very physical job and what better ownership of the cooking process could you have than building the oven, mastering the fire and then truly wanting to cook in it? Move over barbecues, brick ovens are the next dimension.

Introduction

RUSSELL'S PIZZA
08 8556 2571

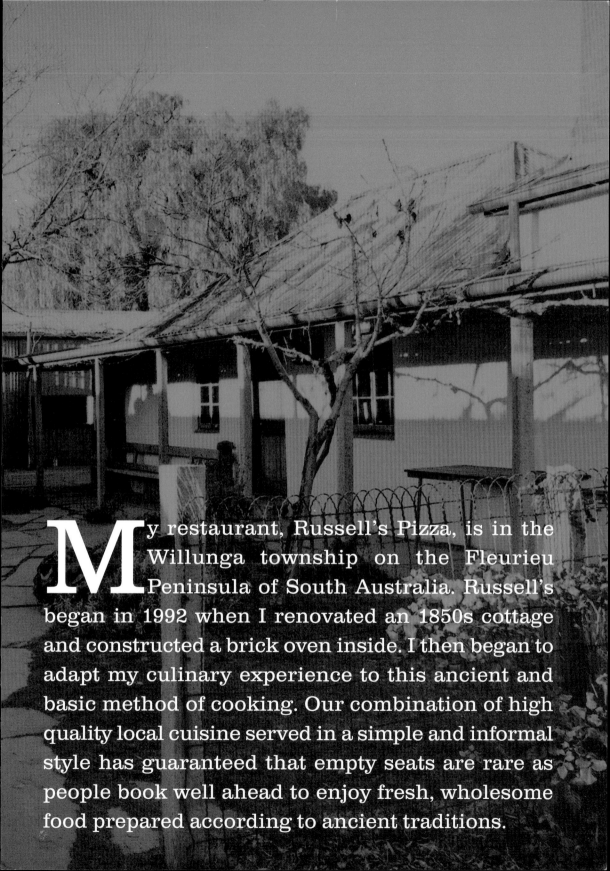

My restaurant, Russell's Pizza, is in the Willunga township on the Fleurieu Peninsula of South Australia. Russell's began in 1992 when I renovated an 1850s cottage and constructed a brick oven inside. I then began to adapt my culinary experience to this ancient and basic method of cooking. Our combination of high quality local cuisine served in a simple and informal style has guaranteed that empty seats are rare as people book well ahead to enjoy fresh, wholesome food prepared according to ancient traditions.

And hardly a week goes by without at least one person pointing to the brick oven in my restaurant and saying,

'I want ONE of THOSE in my backyard'

My usual reply is something like: 'Then all of your mates will come around expecting food, then they'll drink all your beer.' A few agree with me and wander away, but others stay and come up with more questions. Did you build this one? Are they fire bricks? How long does it take to heat up? To my surprise, there are many adventurous individuals who are ready to tackle building their own oven and want serious advice on how to go about it.

Brick-oven building is an ancient tradition. Brick ovens are part of our culture and our history and building one in your backyard generally remains unencumbered by regulations and requires few specific skills. Not only are you free to build a brick oven, you can express yourself by capping it with anything from a witches' hat to an integrated energy system that heats water and your home.

The purpose of this book is not to give you so much information that it quashes your motivation to build. After all, I'm not going to build your oven – you are! Building a brick oven is something that *you* do and that's what it's all about. Your oven won't be perfect, but it will be yours to live and learn with.

I've built four ovens, so I know a few tricks and pointers, and I've been cooking in brick ovens for twelve years at my restaurant in Willunga, and that's where the real adventure lies. Your brick oven will connect you to thousands of years and countless generations of hard work and happy cooks.

A brick oven provides us with a glimpse into the evolution of cookery. When we use our ovens we can begin to understand the economic, ecological and cultural roots of the dishes that we enjoy today. Many of the rules of cookery have sprung from the problems and limitations experienced by those before us. So when we work with our ovens we become part of something larger than ourselves and our delusions of mastery. The oven calls us to pay attention and raise a sweat but through our commitment to this ancient tool we are repaid again and again, and not just with a good lunch, although a good lunch is enough.

Brick oven at Pompeii, Italy – at least 2000 years old

Part One

Building Your Oven

What is a brick oven? Brick ovens come in many shapes and sizes but they all share basic characteristics. A chamber is constructed from bricks to create a fireplace and a mass to store the heat from the fire built inside.

BUILDING your OVEN

The main objective is to efficiently store the heat and utilise it primarily for the purpose of cooking. The cooking takes place in the same chamber where the fire  is lit. Sometimes we cook with the fire inside the chamber at the same time. In this case the oven door is left open to release the smoke. At other times, the fire is removed and the heat retained by the bricks is used for cooking.

Building Your Oven

STAGE 1:
The Base

A brick oven works by drawing air through the lower part of the door at the front and exhausting it out through the upper part into the atmosphere. The design of the oven guarantees that the heat-laden post-combustion air has maximum contact with the brick surface area inside the oven before it leaves. This is the objective of all managed combustion, and explains why there is no chimney on top and only one hole in the front of the oven.

We are building a brick oven not a wood oven. Most of the cooking advantages of a brick oven come from the heated bricks and not the wood, and the quality of the food is not enhanced by the character of the wood you're burning or the presence of smoke, so a good brick oven hardly makes any smoke. The better your fire and drier the wood, the less smoke it will make.

Where should you build your brick oven? Brick ovens can be built inside, outside or semi-outdoors.

Let's start outside in a typical backyard.

If you live in a dry climate or plan to use your oven infrequently, or, for whatever reason, you chose to build it in the open air, the problem of getting the smoke away is greatly reduced (*figure 1*). It may be enough to consider the prevailing winds and potential fire hazards and site the oven accordingly. Certainly site the oven at least two metres from anything combustible and well clear of bushland.

Figure 1: A free-standing oven in the open air can be a very basic oven

If you build your oven inside a building, then a flue or chimney must be incorporated into the design and choice of location (a flue is the metal tube used to extract smoke from the oven). The difference of air pressure between the inside of the building and the outside will mean the smoke is sucked outside through a properly designed flue or chimney. This is absolutely critical to ensure no smoke or gases escape into living areas, especially if you are burning wood (*figure 2*).

Somewhere in between these two possibilities is an oven built in a semi-outdoors location, say in a courtyard or under a veranda. In this situation it is important to direct the smoke away, but we don't have the advantage of the pressure variation between inside and outside a building to create the suction that helps a chimney work well. In this situation, no matter how well you build your chimney, it is likely that some of the smoke will escape and blow about. This problem can be overcome by making sure that there is plenty of air flow through the area, maintaining a good clean fire and incorporating a carefully designed and effective flue (*figure 3*).

Figure 2

Figure 3

8 Building Your Oven

An understanding of the behaviour of smoke will help you decide where to build your oven. Basically, if you build in a favourite corner of the garden or down by the creek, you may not need a flue or chimney. If you want the oven under cover where people will gather close to the house, you need to consider smoke control carefully. When you build your oven right inside a building, a functional chimney will solve your smoke problems.

The oven is built in four stages: the base, the oven dome, the flue and an enclosure for insulation and any other additions. Where you locate your oven will determine whether or not you need to build all four stages. For a free-standing, open-air oven you can get away with stage one and two and then start cooking – an attractive choice for those of you who are impatient to fire up and get on with it! (*figure 4*)

Interior oven with old tank for insulation cavity

Figure 4: The four stages of building

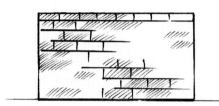

Base

Base and basic oven

1 | 2
3 | 4

Base, oven and flue

Base, oven, flue, insulation cavity
and hot water pipes

10 Building Your Oven

I will describe the four stages one by one in the following pages. We will be building a simple dome-shaped design with an interior measurement of 1100 millimetres. You can certainly build your oven smaller or bigger according to your situation. A 1100 millimetre oven is an ideal size for a backyard party oven.

There are no rules for building the base for your oven, so you may as well demonstrate whatever skills or talents you possess, using whatever materials you choose or have handy. Here are a few examples from creative oven makers (*figures 5.1–5.6*).

The front edge of the base needs to be at least 100 millimetres clear of the oven door. If you have more space, 200 millimetres makes it easier to add your insulation cladding later. If a flue is required, allow 300 millimetres. More than 400 millimetres will make access to the oven awkward.

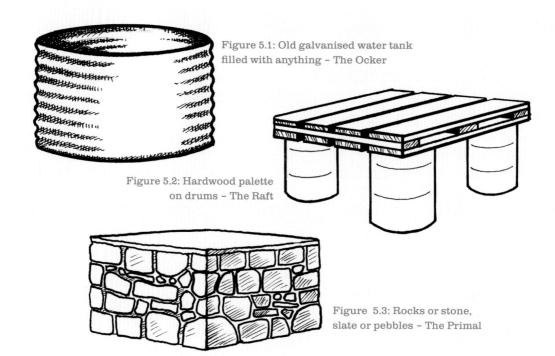

Figure 5.1: Old galvanised water tank filled with anything – The Ocker

Figure 5.2: Hardwood palette on drums – The Raft

Figure 5.3: Rocks or stone, slate or pebbles – The Primal

Extending the base to include a working surface or a barbecue hearth for burning coals can be very useful. If you want to get really fancy, design a cavity underneath for wood or tools storage.

The area where the most potential for creativity lies is in the front where the door will be. The main innovation I have worked on is an ash box, especially for an indoor oven (*figure 6*).

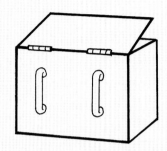

Figure 6: Ash box for storing ash and coals made out of 3 millimetre steel with a flat sliding lid or hinged lid at the front top. A cavity for receiving the ash box will need to be built into the base

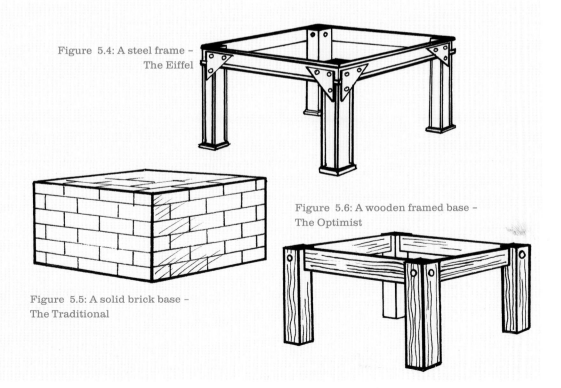

Figure 5.4: A steel frame – The Eiffel

Figure 5.6: A wooden framed base – The Optimist

Figure 5.5: A solid brick base – The Traditional

Building Your Oven

Figure 7

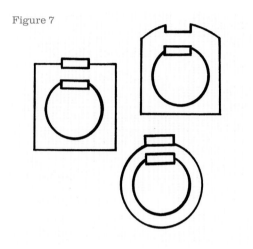

Figure 8

Reinforced cement

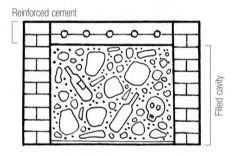

Filled cavity

Figure 9

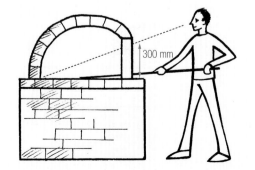

300 mm

The base can be any shape as long as it is bigger than the proposed circumference of your oven. Basically, it has to support half a ton of weight in bricks (*figure 7*).

The bases of my ovens are filled with rocks and sand up to 100 millimetres below the rim. The top layer is made of compacted sand or reinforced cement with perlite mixed in as aggregate to create an insulating effect (*figure 8*).

The height of the base can be anywhere between table and bar height. Mine are a metre high but it depends on how tall you are. I recommend you build to a height that prevents you having to bend over to see what is happening inside (*figure 9*).

I like to be able to see the rear of the oven floor when standing about a metre from the base. This way I can be standing by, chatting with a drink, and just a glance will reveal what's going on in the oven. Remember to take the height of the door into consideration. Allow for the thickness of the floor – or sole of the oven – when working out the height of the base.

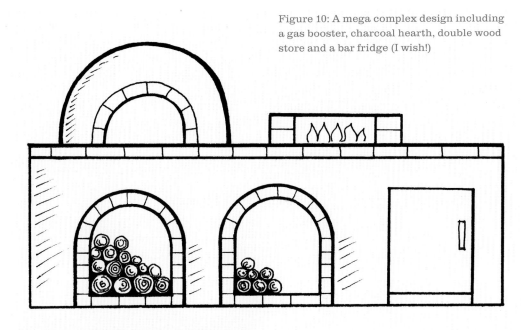

Figure 10: A mega complex design including a gas booster, charcoal hearth, double wood store and a bar fridge (I wish!)

Figure 11: The diameter, or width, of the base of my oven is 1500 millimetres. This allows space to build outer walls later. It includes a box section for the ash box

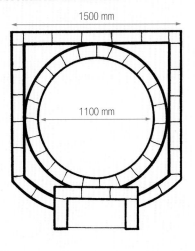

1500 mm

1100 mm

This job is going to be a lot easier if you have one of the following: a brick-cutting machine, a handy mate with a brick-cutting machine, access to a brick-cutting machine, an angle grinder (six-inch is safer) with a diamond blade, a handy mate with an angle grinder and diamond blade, your partner for life with a hammer and bolster.

STAGE 2:
The Dome

You will need one hundred and fifty bricks, although, to be honest, I've never counted them. I use pressed reds, but any brick will do. If you want to spend money for no good reason, use fire bricks if you must, but they are designed for kilns, not ovens. A brick is fired at 1100°C and is stable until your oven reaches that temperature, which it won't unless you're a pyromaniac from hell and you want to cook pizza in a second. Your oven is unlikely to get hotter than 600°C and that is when it is really fired up.

In describing the next process I am going to impart several secrets that will help you proceed with confidence. All you need is the will, so start thinking of fresh-baked bread and your favourite pizza about now.

16 Building Your Oven

Figure 12

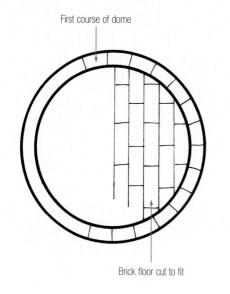

First course of dome

Brick floor cut to fit

Figure 13

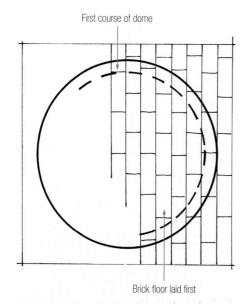

First course of dome

Brick floor laid first

For an oven that is going to get a lot of use, especially a commercial one, I recommend building the first course of the dome and then cutting-in the floor so it is replaceable if it wears out (*figure 12*). (Note that this will add the height of the first course of bricks to the height of the floor of the oven.)

For an oven that won't be used that often, lay the floor on top of the base and simply build the dome on top. This way some of the floor bricks will stick out under the walls of the oven – easier to build, harder to replace the floor (*figure 13*). If you do it this way, make sure your brick floor is stable, even and flat before building the dome. I always butt join the floor bricks – I don't use mortar between them.

Upgraded floor possibilities might include selecting floor bricks with smooth melted tops, using large square refractory bricks, or laying the bricks on their sides to gain extra mass and a smoother floor. My outside oven has two layers of clay pavers. The first layer is a base and gives extra mass, and the second forms the sole of the oven. This way it is easy to replace damaged parts of the floor because the bricks are thinner and easy to cut. Also I found that the pavers had smoother tops than the house bricks I used for the dome *(figure 14)*.

I recommend a steel form or arch door frame that is integrated into your oven as you build. Have it made at your local metal fabricator or bash out your own *(figure 15)*.

The following dimensions are for a 1100 millimetre oven.

To form the circle and dome shape you will need a dome gauge. This is a useful tool for forming the circle and dome shape of your oven and is simple to make. The length of the rod will be the radius of your oven. Mine is 550 millimetres long. The right-angle section is designed to cup the brick while you lay it in position. The end of the rod will require a point in the middle

Figure 14

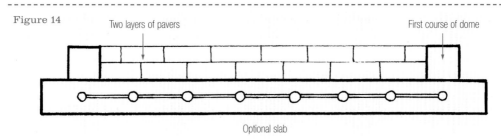

Two layers of pavers

First course of dome

Optional slab

Figure 15

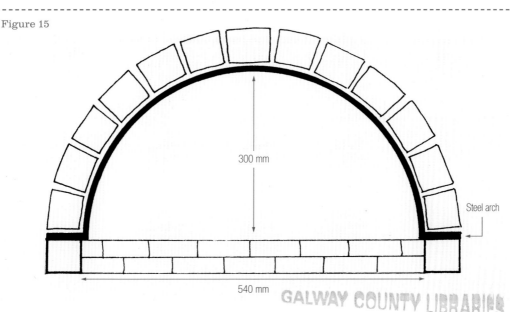

300 mm

Steel arch

540 mm

18

of the floor to swing from. You can figure out how to do that. I used a large washer secured in position with nails *(figure 16)*.

The dome is laid with half bricks cut with a bolster (a chisel with a wide cutting edge, used for cutting stone) or a brick-cutting machine. Do not bother cutting them if you do not have a machine, as it doesn't matter if they are rough on the outside. For an 1100 millimetre oven you will need about one hundred whole bricks.

A standard brick-laying mortar is suitable for the dome; for example, one part cement, one part lime to six parts brick sand. The brick sand is important because it contains clay so it behaves more like a brick under the temperature variations. Fire clay can also be added to further stabilise the mortar, but it is hard to get and not vital. As with most brick mortar,

Figure 16

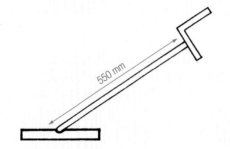

Figure 17

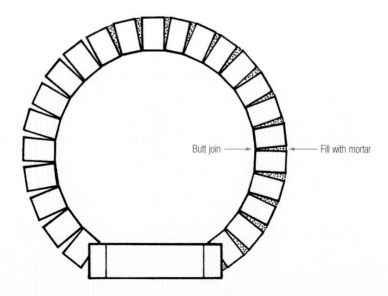

Butt join → ← Fill with mortar

a little detergent will make it creamier – a capful per barrow. Your mortar needs to be on the slightly dry side to minimise shrinkage from moisture loss. Remember it is a brick oven, not a mortar oven, so don't be too concerned about getting the mortar exactly right.

Lay the first course of the dome by butting the bricks on the inside and filling them in from behind with the mortar. The first course can be laid level and will determine the shape of your oven (*figure 17*).

If you're making an oven with a replaceable floor, the floor can now be laid, min- imising the brick cutting required. Next place your arched steel door frame in position and lay an arch of half-length bricks over the top using the steel as support (*see figure 15*). A neater arch is achieved if the bricks are cut into wedges.

When it comes time to lay the second course, the bricks will begin to turn towards the inside. The dome gauge will hold the brick in position for a few moments while the mortar grabs. Where possible, lay the bricks over the joints of the previous course, same as when building a wall (*figure 18*).

Figure 18

First course

Building Your Oven

The first course of bricks will need to line up with the outside of the door arch. Each successive course will meet the arch further towards the centre of the oven. Hopefully, with some adaptation if needed, the bricks will meet at the top of the arch. Cut the bricks to interlock with the arch, especially at the top. It may be necessary to elongate the shape of the oven to marry properly with the top of the door arch (*figure 19*).

I would suggest that you lay up your oven in one good busy day, but it is not vital to do so. When you have raised the dome to the point where gravity will pull the bricks out of position the dome will need support from the inside so you can finish. I use a pile of boxes and a plywood disk to support a light mortar (8:1) dome cap acting as a mould. Let the mortar dome set for an hour before completing the oven (*figure 20*).

As you finish the dome, use your off-cut bricks to fill any uneven gaps. Later, when the boxes are removed you can tidy up the inside of the dome cap by tapping bricks either in or out. You have to get inside the oven to do this.

On completion of the dome, tie it all together with a coating of mortar sufficient to even up the outside. Resist firing for at least a few hours and dont worry about it cracking when you do.

Figure 19

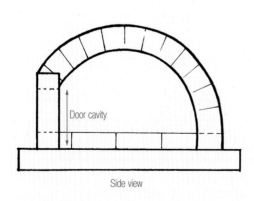

Side view

Figure 20: Finishing the dome

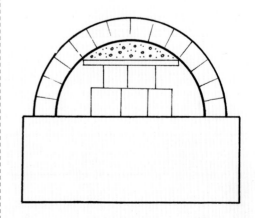

Certainly, by the next day, you can use your oven but you will need a door for baking bread. The door stops air flowing through the oven and cooling it once the fire is removed. Doors come in many forms. The simplest is a piece of plywood cut to the same shape but slightly larger than the door arch. For greater durability I suggest a steel door with a folded edge at the bottom to provide stability. Insulating your door is beneficial for preventing heat loss and this can be achieved by bolting timber onto the steel door or by making a cavity steel door and filling it with purlite (a manufactured volcanic rock commonly used for hydroponics that is heat stable, light and excellent for insulation) or some other material with insulating qualities. The door is clamped onto the door arch of the oven by simply leaning a brick against it. When the door isn't in use it can sit neatly in some stirrups built into your oven's base (*figure 21*).

Figure 21a: A plywood or timber door

Figure 21b: A steel door with a bottom lip for stability. Bolt plywood on the front side for extra insulation

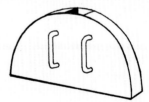

Figure 21c: Cavity steel door with a hole in the top to pour in some insulating material

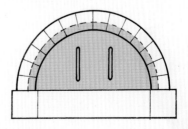

Figure 21d: Oven door arch showing door 10 millimetres larger to allow clamping and sealing against the arch

STAGE 3:
The Flue

There are many ways to flue your oven. I will assume your oven is indoors, as all the same principles apply to a veranda or courtyard oven.

STAGE 3:
The Flue

There will be regulations in place governing the installation of chimneys and flues in your local building code. These are designed to minimise the fire risk in your building and must be complied with to protect yourself and others, and your insurance cover.

You have to decide whether to build a brick chimney, a steel flue or a combination of both. You also have to decide how you will integrate your outer skin into the flue and whether to do it at the same time, especially if you build in brick. A brick flue, of course, will be heavier and may require building approval.

Brick smoke chamber connecting to a steal flue via an old upside-down bucket

Building Your Oven

However you incorporate your smoke chamber, allow room for the oven door (which will be slightly larger than the door cavity) to pass through the chamber and clamp against the door arch. This is critical for sealing your oven when baking bread.

A fabricated steel smoke chamber with flue flange can be bolted to the door arch or welded to the steel arch support *(figure 22a)*.

My preferred method is to build in brick to enclose the dome and change to a steel flue from there. To use this method you need to have allowed at least 200 millimetres of base in front of the door arch, preferably more *(figure 22b)*.

The hot gasses leave the oven at the top of the door arch and naturally head up. The task of the flue is to create an updraft to assist upward flow and, in the case of an indoor oven, to eliminate any chance that gasses will leak into the room. Creating a cavity directly in front of the oven door gets the process started *(figure 23)*.

A good flue needs to start with a smoke chamber with greater dimensions than the upper part. Plan your oven location carefully, so whatever method you use avoids having to angle your flue. Straight up and out is best.

Figure 22a

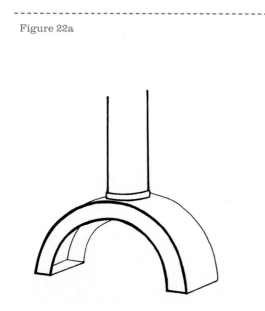

Figure 22b

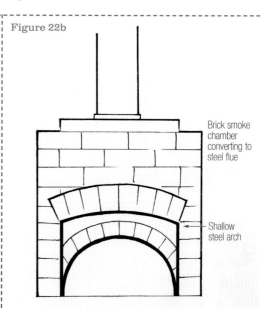

Brick smoke chamber converting to steel flue

Shallow steel arch

Stage 3: The Flue

Your brick smoke chamber will marry well in structure and appearance to your oven. It can be incorporated into raised brick walls to achieve stage four, the insulation cavity, or it can be built independently. I have included the dimensions of my brick smoke chamber, but yours may be different. Just make sure the front arch is low enough to prevent gasses passing the cavity and spilling out the front, and that it starts bigger and ends up smaller.

To convert to steel, I suggest a fabricated flange section to ensure a smooth transition. The flange section needs to be well sealed to the brick section. If the oven is indoors, this seal will be critical. You can use mortar or fire sealing cement and finish with silicone on the outside.

The flange section has to be accurately made to fit the flue snugly inside the flange so water and soot fall inside the chimney *(figure 24)*. We use a 7-inch flue for a 1100 millimetre diameter oven.

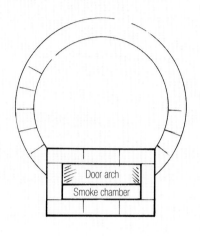

Figure 23: Brick collection chamber constructed over the oven door arch

Door arch

Smoke chamber

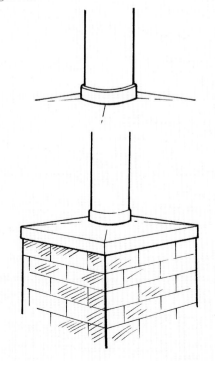

Figure 24

STAGE 4: The INSULATION Cavity

Insulating your oven will help to conserve firewood and ensure your oven performs efficiently. It will warm up more quickly and stay hotter longer. If the oven is indoors, you will be able to control how much heat enters your living space. When you fire your oven, the bricks absorb heat until they reach 'soak' when they can't absorb any more heat. The greater their mass, the greater the heat they absorb. After they are soaked, the bricks give back and reflect heat.

Stage 4: The Insulation Cavity

Figure 25

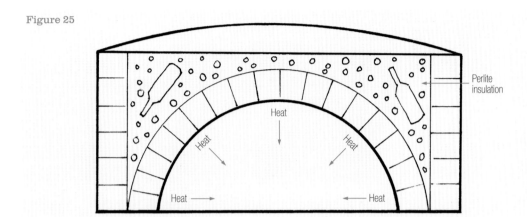

With an insulated oven, the heat is radiated back into the oven without any loss to the atmosphere (*figure 25*).

From a cook's point of view, insulation is very important. I would urge the creative builder to not compromise on insulation as your design evolves. The best result is when you can put your hand on the outer wall of your oven and not feel heat.

This can be achieved by allowing at least an average of 200 millimetres of purlite filling. Purlite, commonly used in hydroponic gardening, is a manufactured volcanic-type rock, similar to natural pumice. It is stable at high temperatures and creates the air barrier required. In the larger areas that need to be filled you can throw in empty bottles to save on cost.

You will need to cap the insulation cavity if your oven is in the weather or needs to be kept tidy in a living area. If your oven is behind a wall and well sheltered, it may be better to maintain access. Mine are capped with a thin layer of cement with a bird wire mesh to minimise cracking.

Stage 2 original inside oven at Russell's

Stage 3 and 4, same oven

Oven at Coriole Vineyard, McLaren Vale, built into a wall with an adjacent open fireplace (page 19)

The first course laid on top of the floor (page 19)

Steel arch for the door (page 17)

Sand mould ready to build the dome cap (page 20)

Using an alternative dome gauge to construct the dome – this one is made from plywood (page 18)

Adjusting the dome cap bricks (page 20)

Oven at Coriole Vineyard, McLaren Vale

Firing your Brick Oven

There are two types of firing. The first and most traditional is a 'baking day' firing. For a baking day a full firing is required, resulting in well-soaked bricks and a great mass of retained heat. Then the fire is removed, the oven cleaned and the retained heat used to cook the food. The idea is to use all of the heat that is created. Before the days of fossil fuels and machinery such as chainsaws, gathering fuel was time consuming so a good housekeeper or baker was not about to waste it. A repertoire of baked items and dishes evolved to utilise each phase of oven heat. This is just as important today because one of the great pleasures of using a brick oven is how it demonstrates the development of our culinary traditions. Economy is as important today as it has ever been, and remains one of the backbone principles of good cooking.

36 Building Your Oven

An example of a sequence of dishes cooked in order after a good firing might include roast vegetables with pizza for lunch, followed by a full oven of breads, perhaps a roast of meat or a slow-cooked stew, a baked pudding, cake or pie, then, as the oven continues to cool, baked custards, shortbreads, roasted nuts, and later, yoghurt, meringues and dried herbs. Then climb in yourself to warm up!

In cold regions, ovens have been built with beds above them. My ovens have copper pipe coiled around the domes that connect to the hot water system, minimising our use of electricity.

The other type of firing I will call a 'party fire'. At a party you might not cook anything, instead using your oven for heating or atmosphere. But you might make some pizzas, meat balls, a baked fish or some roast vegies. The fire is kept going inside the oven to provide direct heat and light, as well as using the heat being radiated from the soaked bricks. You may even just fire your oven to create a bed of coals to grill a steak for lunch with no intention

Copper pipe for heating water coiled around the dome

of heating up the greater oven. This type of firing is used to cook items that are ready to eat, require a high temperature and/or a short cooking time.

Originally pizza was cooked in a very hot oven before loaves of bread were loaded in. A traditional pizza was a thin disc made using a piece of spare dough that would cook in the ferocious heat in a matter of seconds and provide a welcome snack for the family at the beginning of baking day. The ovens seen in commercial pizza restaurants are a good example of a party oven where the fire is kept constantly hot, ready to cook hundreds of pizzas and other dishes without using the stored heat afterwards.

A typical party firing may occur on a Sunday in the backyard. The fire is lit in the morning, ingredients are prepared, the dough is made and a table set for pressing out pizza. The guests arrive and after a drink, begin making pizzas and peeling them into the oven themselves. This can go on all day, and is a great activity that can include the children and shares the job of feeding everyone.

Building Your Oven

You'll need a few basic tools to fire your oven. I suggest an old hoe for poking the fire, a mop and a peel to get started. A peel is a flat spade-like tool used to insert and remove items from the oven. You may be able to buy one at a catering supplier, otherwise you will have to make one or have it made at a sheet metal fabricator. A cheap banister broom screwed onto a long handle is also very useful. You will work out what you need as you go along and a little improvisation will go a long way.

An old grain shovel is useful for moving coals from your oven to wherever you are going to store them until they are cold. Building an ash box into the front of your door can solve this problem. I have an old galvanised rubbish bin in the courtyard to

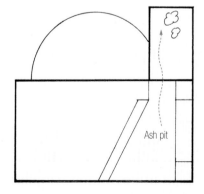

Figure 26

Ash pit

store burning ashes. Traditional indoor areas would often have an ash pit under the oven with a separate flue for this purpose. After the ashes had gone cold they could be safely moved from the building *(figure 26)*.

Hopefully you will have an outside tap with a drain or a domestic sink where you can clean your mop. A mop bucket will do, but it is a messy business.

To fire the oven you will need a source of fuel. I am amazed when I think back to all the fuel that has come my way. One time, three truckloads of assorted off-cuts of wood arrived after a council order was given to a hoarder to clean up his yard. I've burnt cardboard boxes, olive pressings, building off-cuts, fence posts, packing cases. You get an eye for it after a while. Of course, clean split seasoned firewood or mallee roots are preferable, but don't be afraid to get your oven going with whatever comes your way.

Traditional faggots are a useful unit of fuel. Made from gathered sticks bundled together and tied, they can be various sizes and grades of sticks. They are great for shoving in the oven and fire quickly into an inferno due to the large surface area of fuel. For bread, a number of faggots may be sufficient to reheat the oven if it is still warm from the day before.

For an average firing, two wheelbarrows of wood will be required. Get the fire going, hot and furious to start, and keep a good fire until you reach soak. For making great bread, you need a well soaked and very hot oven. It may take up to two hours to achieve this from a cold start, especially in winter.

Be sure to move your fire around to heat the floor and walls evenly unless you specifically want to create hot spots and cold areas.

Part Two

Most of the dishes in the following section can be cooked in your brick oven. For the dishes that are partly prepared in saucepans, rake some coals to the front of your fire

Cooking in Your Oven

and use them to cook over. Be patient with yourself, cooking over coals takes some skill, especially for the delicate dessert dishes. Of course, you can always cheat and use your stove top for guaranteed results and save your oven for the baking phase.

Soak your oven with a good hot fire. This will take several hours if it is cold and a much shorter time if it is warm from the day before. The fire needs to be managed to avoid intense hot spots, so keep it moving around the floor and remove the ash as you go. The key to a good fire is plenty of air so rearrange your fuel to allow air to flow through the fire.

Preparing Your Oven for Baking Bread

When the bread loaves are nearly ready to load into the oven (see recipe on page 46), clean out the coals to a safe place. (I use a steel rubbish bin standing inside a heat guard – an upright 44-gallon drum which has had both ends removed.) Clean the oven floor with a damp (not wet) mop and a brush screwed to the end of a stick. Toss in some flour to test the floor. You will soon see where it is too hot because the flour will burn instantly. Cool the hot spots with a slightly wetter mop dragged over the floor.

After making bread for most of my life and baking in brick ovens for fifteen years, I still find bringing the oven and the rising loaves together challenging – the timing must be perfect, but that is the thrill of baking.

When everything is ready to go, use cloths to flip the loaves gently onto the floured peel then slide them directly onto the oven floor, starting at the rear and avoiding any remaining hot spots. You can slash the loaves with a razor or a serrated knife if you want to increase expansion. Don't worry if you can't set up the loaves perfectly, just get them in and get the door in place.

Now the magic happens. At the right temperature, the water trapped inside the protein structure of the dough begins its conversion to steam and a massive expansion takes place as the liquid becomes gas. If the oven is too cold the loaves cook without this process occurring, making flat, soggy, heavy loaves. If the oven is too hot, the crust

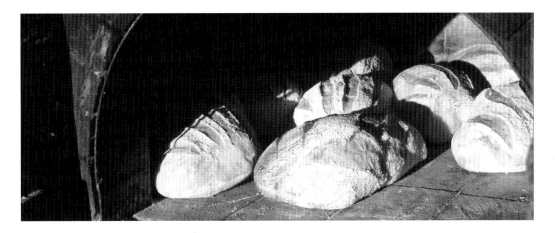

forms too quickly and the loaves can't expand with the same result. When the temperature is just right, expansion, or 'kick', is maximised before the crust is formed and cooking completed.

Now for the moment that no brick oven baker ever tires of – the first glimpse of your results. Whatever happens, each oven load will inspire you to improve your performance. If the loaves are pale, seal the oven back up. If they are burning, leave the door open. Half an hour will usually be long enough to cook the bread. It is ready when the crust is well formed and coloured and they sound hollow when knocked. Great loaves will have a lightness when you handle them. Set them in a basket or on a wire rack to cool.

Now you have made basic hand-made loaves cooked directly on the bricks. To make specialty loaves, wholemeal loaves, French sticks, croissants and hot-cross buns use your favourite recipes but remember, like many things in this world, moisture management is the key to achieving the best results.

Recipes

Cooking in Your Oven

Bread (makes eight loaves)

Brick ovens work best on a full load of bread because of the steaming effect they create inside. Halve or quarter the quantities below to make four or only two loaves at a time.

3 kg unbleached bread flour
1 kg Stoneground wholemeal
   flour (we use biodynamic 80%
   light which has the courser
   bran sifted out)
1 tsp dried yeast
2 tbsp salt
1250 ml rain or filtered water

Mix the flour and yeast on a table and form a well in the middle. Dissolve the salt in half a litre of boiling water, then add the rest of the water. If the ingredients are cold the water needs to be hotter. (We are working towards body temperature dough.) Pour the water into the well using one hand to gather in the flour to make a paste first and then a dough. Keep one hand free for adding more water or flour. When the dough is cohesive but wet and sticky, begin to knead with both hands. Keep a plastic pastry scraper handy to scrape the dough from the table and your hands. Continue folding and turning until a smooth, cohesive, easy to work dough has formed.

Place the dough in a steep-sided container like a bucket or pot. If it is cold, put it somewhere warm. If it is very cold, put it in a sink of warm water. Cover with oiled plastic and a blanket. I use a foil space blanket from the camping shop.

For bread, dough will require a long proving. Leave it to rise to double its size. This could take up to five hours, leaving plenty of time to fire your oven. For pizza, the dough can be used straight away, but results will be better the longer it proves.

To make loaves, once the dough has risen, turn it out and divide it into eight portions. Using a minimum of flour, form the loaves by folding the dough in on itself. Aim to achieve a large surface area – thinner, longer, wider – rather than rounder, taller, thicker. The dough must be moist, loose and feisty to handle. Avoid overworking the dough at this stage – just work to get the loaves in shape in good time so they all rise again together. I recommend an elongated shape about as wide as your hand. This shape works best flat on the oven floor.

Lay the well-floured loaves between cloths ready to be flipped on to the peel later.

The second proving will be quicker because the dough is well conditioned and still light with gasses. It is important that they are loaded into the hot oven with room to expand, so have your oven ready before they are fully risen. If you imagine the loaves are your lungs taking a big breath, they need to go in the oven at two-thirds the way to being full. Cover the loaves with your space blanket while they rise in a warm, draught-free place.

For best results

- Use best quality flour.
- Moisture is critical. Incorporate as much moisture as possible while still forming a cohesive mass for kneading.
- Learn to adjust the water temperature so the dough ends up at body temperature, but cooler is better than hotter.

Pizza Dough

For pizza, use the same dough recipe as for bread, but you will need to use more flour to prevent it sticking to your bench and peel.

Pizza cooked directly on the hot bricks gives the best results. It is pizza-making tradition to save some dough from the bread mix before the second proving. The dough is pressed out thin, topped with a few simple ingredients and cooked in the oven after the fire is removed. This way the ferocious initial heat is used and the baker has an excellent lunch – a good way to encourage helpers.

More and more ovens are fired just for pizza making. In this case, fire the oven as for bread but leave a good fire to one side when you clean the floor. You may want to use the hot spots to get crispy bases on your pizzas. Great flat breads and pocket breads can be made using the same dough. As for the skill of peeling the pizzas from the bench to the oven and back – you will have to figure that out for yourself.

For best results

- Make small pizzas to begin with.
- Don't crowd the toppings. Leave some patches with no sauce or topping so the base cooks from the top as well as the bottom.
- Move the pizzas around to release moisture and pick up more heat from the bricks.
- Cook them quickly so the toppings remain fresh.
- Use best quality ingredients sparingly.

Hands are best!

Cooking in Your Oven

Napoli Pizza (makes one pizza)

Ah, Napoli! How can a city be so beautiful and so mad at the same time? Embraced by the awesome Mount Vesuvius and the Bay of Naples, Napoli is a crazy metropolis congested with traffic, buildings, people and great, great food. The pizza-making lesson from the metropolis is to keep it simple – the streets might be crowded but the pizza is far from it. Use a hot oven, and wonderful evocative buffalo mozzarella. Our version isn't authentic, but it's certainly inspired by the great cooks of Napoli.

^{1}/2 cup black olives
250 g prepared dough
olive oil
^{1}/2 cup fresh tomato sauce
    (tomato cooked and strained)
^{1}/2 cup fresh tomatoes, diced
fresh basil
1 tbsp parmesan cheese
150 g buffalo mozzarella,
    sliced 1 centimetre thick

First remove the pips from the olives and make a paste. You can add a little fresh garlic and a few drops of balsamic vinegar if you like. Do it with a mortar and pestle or use a food processor.

Press out the dough and brush it with olive oil. Spread the tomato sauce but not too evenly. Sprinkle on the fresh diced tomatoes, basil and the parmesan cheese. Place the mozzarella in rounds. Put some blobs of olive paste in three or four places.

Cook the pizza fast to avoid spoiling the mozzarella with overcooking. Serve it with fresh basil and a drizzle of olive oil.

Anchovy Special (makes one pizza)

A version of the French Pissaladiere, this is how we deal with those kinky anchovy people. Anchovy haters should skip this one or leave the anchovies out. Anchovy lovers, read on. The sweet onions and salty olives and anchovies will bring out the best in your crisp white and sparkling wines. We use a fresh tin of anchovies for each pizza as they deteriorate very quickly after the tin is opened.

1 large onion, sliced
olive oil
1 red capsicum
1 zucchini, small to medium
pepper and salt
250 g prepared dough
1/2 cup seeded black olive halves
    (good ones! with flavour!)
1 x 25 g tin of anchovies
    in olive oil
chopped parsley

Sweeten the sliced onion in 3 tablespoons of olive oil in a small pot over low heat. They should be soft, creamy and sweet, but not caramelised. Cut the four sides off the capsicum and slice the zucchini into 5 millimetre long ways strips. Toss the zucchini strips and capsicum in a bowl with a little oil and pepper and salt, then lay them on a roasting tray and cook fast over coals raked to the front of your oven. The aim is to use sufficient heat to colour them on both sides without overcooking. This is an essential brick-oven skill also used to cook vegetables like eggplant, zucchini, capsicums, pumpkin and fennel bulb. Tear the capsicum into strips 1 centimetre wide.

Press out your dough and spread on the sliced onions. Place the vegetable strips with kinks and the olives pushed down into the onion. Open the tin of anchovies and lay them around. Season with salt and pepper. After cooking, sprinkle with chopped parsley for the essential fresh finish.

Lamb Turkish

We use lamb to make the filling, but any meat will do. Turkish-style pide are long and folded at the edges to enclose all kinds of fillings. A bit tricky to prepare, but easy to cook and they don't require a very hot oven.

For the filling
(makes enough for two or three)

1 onion, diced
2 tbsp olive oil
500 g minced lamb
500 g diced lamb for stewing
water, stock or wine to barely
    cover
1 tbsp sweet paprika
1 tbsp cumin
pepper and salt

Cook the onion in the olive oil until it is soft. Add the mince and dice and barely cover it with water, stock or wine. Simmer the meat until the dice is tender. You may have to add moisture, but you don't want it to be wet when it is finished cooking. Add the spices and pepper and salt and allow to cool.

For the pide (makes enough for one)

250 g prepared dough
2 cups cooked meat
$^1/_2$ cup fresh tomato, diced
1 tbsp parsley, chopped
1 tbsp mint, chopped
1 pickled lemon or lime or a
    fresh lemon or lime
2 tbsp yoghurt (we use sheep's)

Press the dough out into an elongated oval shape. Spread on the meat and fold the edge over, but not too much. Pinch along the edges so the sides stand up when it cooks. The ends will be pointy. Cook in a quieter part of the oven until the dough is done. Top with the fresh tomato, parsley, mint, the chopped pickled lemon or lime or fresh juice and a dob of yoghurt on top.

Roast Chicken with English Pan Gravy

The method described here is useful for any kind of roast.

First, rub a chicken inside and out with olive oil, pepper and salt (4 parts salt to 1 part pepper), fresh thyme, lemon rind and garlic. This is called the 'holy trinity' of cooking – olive oil, salt and pepper for taste, aromatics for flavour.

Select a roasting pan made from stainless steel or enamelled cast iron preferably, but aluminium will do. Place the chicken on a bed of parsley stalks, celery, diced onion and anything else that will add flavour. The roast can be cooked in a brick oven with or without a fire. Either way it is best to start it off in a hot oven and allow the heat to reduce gradually.

Cooking in Your Oven

When the chicken is cooked, set it aside to rest in a warm place. What remains in the pan is a mixture of cooked aromatics, juices, fats and herbs. Stir and scrape these precious ingredients over a medium flame or hot coals raked to the front of your oven while the moisture evaporates. When all the water has gone, the bubbling will stop and the temperature of the remaining fat will start to rise. Fat doesn't evaporate, it just keeps getting hotter until it bursts into flames, so pay attention and don't answer the phone. You can develop extra flavour and colour by frying the remaining solids in the clarified fat for one minute, but be careful not to let it burn. You now have flavour-packed caramelised solids and

clear fat remaining so pour off most of the fat, retaining the solids and 2 tablespoons of fat. Stir in 2 tablespoons of flour and cook it briefly. Now add water or stock back to the pan a little at a time, cooking and stirring constantly until sauce consistency is reached.

You now have a richly flavoured natural gravy, free of fat, and ready to finish with pepper, salt and fresh herbs. You can strain the gravy into a pot to remove the solids.

With practice, you will soon be an expert at using your brick oven in the great tradition of the roast dinner. Serve the chicken with roasted root vegetables and freshly boiled or steamed greens.

Roast pumpkin and zucchini

Olive and Asparagus Frittata
(makes enough for eight as an appetiser)

Spring is announced by the new season's asparagus bursting from the ground, freshly pickled olives and the traditional symbol of new life – eggs! Celebrate with this easy, flexible recipe. Great for an appetiser.

1 large onion
olive oil
1 bunch of asparagus
1 cup new season's black olives
10 eggs
salt and pepper
fresh herbs, oregano, parsley,
    chervil, chives

Slice the onion and cook it with 2 tablespoons of olive oil in a small pot until it is sweet and creamy, but not brown. Trim the asparagus and toss into boiling water for one minute then remove to cold water to cool. Cut the blanched asparagus length ways into quarters. Split the olives in halves and remove the pips.

Combine the eggs with a fork and season with salt and pepper. Mix in the freshly chopped herbs, sweetened onion, asparagus and olives.

Pour the egg mixture into a non-rusting pan lined with silicon paper small enough to make the frittata at least 5 centimetres deep. Cook in a slow oven until it is set. Beware of too much heat, as the eggs will overcook and dry out. Egg dishes test the steady hand of a good cook – be kind to them. The finished frittata should be fresh and juicy.

Allow to cool and set. Refrigerate if it is to be eaten later. Frittata can be served as a meal or cut into small squares for appetisers.

Keftetef (Greek Meatballs)
(makes about forty meatballs)

Simple to make and quick to cook, these Greek-style meatballs made an excellent contrast to pizza when you're fired up for a gathering.

1 onion
juice and rind of one lemon
2 tbsp parsley
2 tbsp mint, chopped
1 egg
1 kg lean minced beef
1 cup bread crumbs

Blend the onions, lemon, parsley, mint and egg in your food processor, or finely dice the onion and then mix in the rest. Mix in the beef and bread crumbs and knead for one minute. Refrigerate for one hour.

Roll the mixture into 4 centimetre balls and lay them out on an oiled tray. Cook them in a hot oven and serve them with fresh mint and yoghurt or tomato sauce. A wonderful variation is to make them a little bit bigger and stuff them with fetta cheese – yum!

Baked Snapper with Leeks and Olives
(makes enough for four)

Snapper is an ideal fish for this dish, but any white flesh fish will do. You will need the whole fish as the head and bones are used to make the sauce.

1 carrot, diced
2 sticks celery, diced
4 bay leaves
parsley and thyme
1 bunch of leeks
2 litres rain or filtered water
1.5 kg whole fish, filleted
1/2 cup flour
1/2 cup butter or olive oil
1 cup of olives, halved with pips
    removed
pepper and salt

To make the stock, put the carrot, celery, bay leaves, parsley stalks, a sprig of thyme and the tops of the leeks in a large stock pot and add 2 litres of rain or filtered water. Bring to the boil, then simmer for 20 minutes on the stove top.

Meanwhile, fillet the fish and wash the head and bones. Add the head and bones

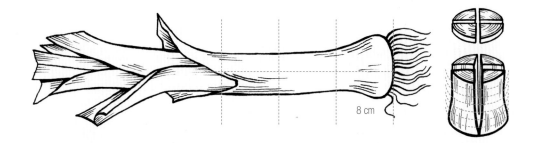

8 cm

to the stock and simmer for as long as it takes for the cooked meat to fall away from the bones. Strain the stock, return the liquid to the pot and continue simmering.

To prepare the leeks, trim the roots but leave the bulb intact. Cut into 8 centimetre lengths and then slice lengthways leaving them still joined

together at the root end. Slice the remaining white of the leek into rounds. Cook the leek in the simmering stock for five minutes before removing it and setting aside.

Make a roux by cooking the flour in the butter or oil for five minutes in a small pot, but don't let it brown. Cool. The stock should by now have reduced to 1.5 litres. Whisk the roux into the stock to thicken and simmer for ten minutes, or longer if it needs to thicken more. Add the leeks, olive halves, pepper and salt and plenty of chopped parsley.

Cut the filleted fish into serve-size pieces and lay them in a baking dish. Pour over the sauce and bake it all in the oven until the fish is cooked and the top is coloured.

You can add fresh oysters or smoked salmon pieces for extra flavour if you like.

Cooking in Your Oven

Vanilla Brandy

Vanilla brandy is used for flavouring pastry cream, crème caramels and cakes. Buy as many fresh, soft, plump vanilla beans as you can, up to half a kilogram. Split the beans longways with a knife, place them in a tall jar and cover them with brandy. Leave for at least a week, but they will keep indefinitely.

Poaching Liquor for Fruit

500 ml orange juice
500 ml white wine
100 g sugar
1 vanilla bean from your vanilla
    brandy jar
$1/2$ tsp cinnamon
orange or lemon rind
10 thin slices of fresh ginger
1 bay leaf
pinch of saffron (optional)
2 nobs of star anise

Combine all the ingredients in a pot and boil for a few minutes. Use this basic poaching liquor to poach pears, quinces, tamarillos, guavas, prickly pears and other late season fruits.

Poached Pears

Trim ripe, but not mushy, pears into quarters and poach them in the poaching liquor for fruit until they soften and become slightly translucent.

Crème Caramel (makes enough for eight)

Crème caramel is a true dessert – light and delicious and without the filling starchy components normally associated with coffee items and puddings – a great dessert for late winter and early spring, before the fruits come into season, and while eggs and milk are at their best.

For the caramel
2 cups of sugar

For the custard
1 litre milk
6 eggs
4 extra egg yolks
2 tbsp vanilla brandy
  (see opposite)
100 g sugar

Caramel can be kept in an airtight container indefinitely, so it is worth making an extra batch while you're at it. You will need a clean, stainless steel or copper pot. Pour in one cup of water, adding the sugar to the centre so it doesn't touch the sides. Place over a medium heat, dissolving the sugar with a minimum of stirring, and bring the mixture to a gentle boil. Wash down the inner sides of

Cooking in Your Oven

the pot with a pastry brush rinsed with plenty of fresh water. Boil off the water, taking great care when evaporation is complete and the temperature starts to climb. Sugar, like fat and oils, just keeps getting hotter until it burns.

When the boiling sugar has caramelised – darkened in colour – remove it from the heat (if it has started smoking you have gone too far) and take it to the sink to rest for one minute. Now, very carefully, drop by drop, add half a cup of

water. The caramel will splutter a bit, but you need to dilute it for easy handling. Return the caramel to the heat and boil in the water. You'll need some practise to achieve a thick but manageable consistency.

To make the custard
Cover the bottom of a ceramic or stainless steel steep-sided oven dish with 3 millimetres of the caramel mixture. Meanwhile, warm the milk enough to dissolve the sugar, then whisk in the other

ingredients and strain. Pour the mixture gently over the caramel. Your crème caramel dish needs to be immersed in water up to the level of the custard while it cooks. We use a large flat-bottomed baking tray for this.

Cook the crème caramel is a slow oven of approximately 150°C. Like all egg dishes it is very heat sensitive and will toughen if the oven is too hot. The time to cook can vary from 30 minutes to an hour.

After cooking, remove from the water bath and cool. The crème caramel will improve for up to a day before turning out. The caramel will draw moisture from the set custard, improving the texture of both the caramel and the custard.

To serve, run a knife around the outside of the crème to loosen it from the pan. Place a plate on top and flip the plate and the pan together. Carefully remove the pan releasing the crème and the custard sauce. It's easier to portion and serve if you use two palette knives or spatulas.

Cooking in Your Oven

Chocolate Cake with Poached Pears

This cake has all the rich flavoursome intensity that made mud cakes so popular, but without the mud. Look no further for the all-round perfect chocolate cake recipe. The key lies in using grated chocolate instead of melted chocolate and tricking the cake into rising and setting before it folds under the weight of the high chocolate content.

250 g chocolate, grated

250 g fine almond meal

1/2 cup of chocolate powder
   (sugar-free cocoa)

1/2 cup of brandy or vanilla
   brandy (see page 62)

12 eggs

200 g caster sugar

Mix the grated chocolate and almond meal together. Make a paste by mixing the chocolate powder and brandy together in a separate bowl.

Separate the eggs, taking care not to get any egg yolk in the whites. Beat the whites until there are no big bubbles and they start to firm. Continue beating and gradually add 150 grams of sugar. Transfer the whites to a large bowl. Now beat the egg yolks, slowly adding the remaining sugar until they are light, pale and creamy.

Add the yolks to the whites and drizzle the brandy and chocolate powder paste over the top. Sprinkle on some almond and chocolate, and fold over the eggs. Continue to sprinkle and fold to incorporate the dry ingredients trying to minimise the loss of air from the mix. Your folding skills and care will be evident in the final result. The last fold takes place as you pour it into the cake tin. You can use a deep tin or a shallow one. We line the bottom with silicon paper.

Bake in a moderate oven until an inserted skewer comes out clean. Cover with paper if it gets too dark on top.

Serve the cake with juicy poached pears (see page 62) and cream if you wish. The cake can be filled with strawberries and cream and/or coated with a ganach made from half cream, half chocolate melted together.

Apple Strudel (makes enough for ten or twelve people)

Apple strudel has the wonderful qualities of being natural, wholesome and low in fat, and utterly delicious with or without cream.

450 g unbleached bread flour

3/4 cup warm water

1 egg

juice and rind of one lemon

2 tbsp olive oil

2 kg apples (Golden Delicious are great because they don't go mushy)

1/2 cup almonds, lightly roasted

1/2 cup currants

1/2 cup raisins

1/2 cup sugar

2 tsp cinnamon

Place the flour on your table and make a well in the centre. Combine the water, egg, lemon juice and oil and pour it into the well. Gather in the sides and make a paste and proceed to make a bread-like dough, adding more water if necessary. Knead it until it is smooth and silky, keeping in mind that, like bread, it is better more wet than dry – but not too wet. Shape a seamless ball and put it aside in a plastic bag.

Skin, core and slice your apples into a bowl. Give the almonds a few chops with a knife and add them to the currants, raisins, sugar, lemon rind and cinnamon.

Assemble the strudel while your bread is baking so it will be ready to go in the medium oven. As with all brick oven management, timing is critical for using the stored heat.

To 'spin' your dough, you will need a large floured surface, preferably accessible from all sides. Pat out the well rested dough and begin rolling it into the largest circle you can, using enough flour to keep it from sticking. Pick up the dough on the back of your knuckles and use its own weight to stretch it into an

Cooking in Your Oven

ever increasing circle until it is very thin and up to a metre across. You can stretch it further by dragging your fingers towards you underneath the dough, even using weights to hold down the opposite side. Persevere, as developing this skill will reap great rewards.

Brush the thin dough with olive oil and spread the apple mixture over the furthest two-thirds of the circle. Trim the thick edge of the dough and roll up your strudel towards the part with no fruit.

Stretch it as you roll, and roll reasonably tightly. The last part of the dough will hold it all together. Place a flat tray next to it and manoeuvre it on with the join downwards and laid out in a zig-zag or oval shape.

Place it in your oven and cook it for about an hour, or until the apple is well cooked. Brush it a few times with oil or cream if you wish.

Serve hot or cold, dusted with icing sugar, with or without cream.

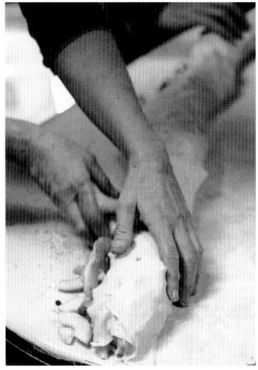

Pastry Cream
(makes about 1.5 litres)

Pastry cream is used as a base to make fillings for tarts, cakes and meringues.

1 litre milk
8 egg yolks
175 g caster sugar
175 g plain flour

Warm the milk on a stove top until it is just too hot to put your finger in. In another bowl beat the egg yolks and slowly add the sugar until the mixture is light and creamy. Add a little of the milk and then mix in the flour to make a smooth batter, then slowly add the rest of the milk.

Cook the mixture over a slow to medium heat on a stove top until it thickens, then continue to cook and stir for at least ten minutes, but longer is better. Don't worry if it is lumpy and add a little more milk if it gets too stiff.

Tart Glaze
(makes 500 millilitres)

1 cup of fruit trimmings
   (peach or pear)
200 ml orange juice
100 ml water
1 tsp sugar
3 leaves of gelatine

Boil the fruit trimmings on a stove top with the orange juice, water and sugar for five minutes and strain. Soak the gelatine leaves in cold water for one minute or until they are soft then squeeze them out and add them to the hot liquid to dissolve. Refrigerate the glaze until it begins to firm, then it is ready for dabbing over your fruit tarts with a pastry brush.

Almond Pastry

(makes two medium-sized tarts)

This is a pressing pastry that is shaped into your tin using your fingers. This requires some skill to achieve an even thickness, but once mastered, it is much easier than rolling out.

120 g butter
75 g icing sugar
40 g almond meal
200 g plain flour

Combine the butter, sugar and almond meal together until light and creamy. Mix in the flour until it is just combined. Alternatively, place all ingredients into a bowl and combine them by rubbing between your fingers. Press out into your tin, aiming for an even thickness. This pastry will keep in the refrigerator for several months.

Strawberry Tart

This classic tart celebrates the first fruits of the spring harvest. That is if you live where the winters are cold.

Using the almond pastry (see page 73) at room temperature, press it into your tart tin with fingers and thumb, no thicker than 3 millimetres, especially through the corners and up the sides. Line the pastry with foil on its own or silicon paper held to the tart's shape with split-pins kept for this purpose. Blind bake in a slow oven. Pay attention as it burns easily. Take out the paper when the sides are set in place and finish cooking to a light golden colour. It doesn't matter how long it takes, and can even be cooked overnight after a day's baking.

Strawberry tart requires a light but firm pastry cream prepared by whisking in one-quarter again of cream to the quantity of your basic pastry cream (see page 71). Mix in your vanilla brandy (see page 62) to taste. Spread it over the base up to 15 millimetres thick according to your preference.

Halve the strawberries if you wish, but whole is best. Arrange them to cover the surface completely, pressing them into the pastry cream to hold them in place. Apply two coats of glaze (see page 71) to marry it all together, refrigerating between coats to set. Be restrained – the glaze is only there to seal and enhance the fruit.

The finished tart is a multi-sensory experience. A brilliant visual unveiling of spring, it also has crunch and the mother's milk luxury of the pastry cream combined with the perfumed flavour and sweet-sour taste of the strawberries.

Sweet Dishes

Peach and Blueberry Tart

Prepare the tart base and pastry cream as for the strawberry tart (see page 74). Peel and halve some fresh, ripe peaches and press them, cut side up, randomly into the pastry cream. Fill the spaces with blueberries. Boil up the peach trimmings to make your glaze (see page 71).

Quince Tart

Cooks love quinces . . . why? Because quinces love cooks. In fact, without a cook, a quince isn't much use. Even the possums leave them to eat last. Some varieties take hours to cook and some cook in fifteen minutes, so you will need to test them. Many cooks transform quinces with large amounts of sugar, creating a spectacular, but very sweet, deep crimson poached fruit. I prefer my quinces lighter and fragrant. This tart is

one way to preserve those qualities and still present a luxurious effect.

First prepare the quinces. Peel and quarter the fruit and cover with poaching liquor (see page 62). You can spice up the liquor with extra thin slices of ginger and a few heads of star anise. Cook the quinces until tender. They can be enjoyed just like this, but for a tart they need a little extra work.

Next lay the quince quarters in rows on a stainless steel baking tray, half covering them with poaching liquor. Slide the tray into a medium-hot oven with the fire going. The radiant direct heat will hopefully colour the quinces with a few dark tips while the liquor reduces and thickens.

Prepare your blind baked tart base with a thin layer of undiluted pastry cream (see page 71). Press the coloured quinces into the cream without leaving spaces. Reduce the liquor further if necessary and spoon it over the quinces.

Return the tart to a slow oven to melt it all together. The result will be a quince tart with a rich, sticky glaze.

Cooking in Your Oven

Almond Meringue
(makes three 30 centimetre flat meringues)

Ideal for using up egg whites (from making pastry cream) and the oven's stored heat after a day's baking. We make batches of meringue overnight and keep them in airtight containers to use later. The same mixture is perfect for piping small 'kisses' which keep indefinitely in a sealed jar.

12 egg whites
400 g caster sugar
1/2 cup almond meal

Beat the whites until there are no large bubbles and the mixture starts to firm. Add the sugar gradually to create a stiff meringue. Fold in the almond meal and spread 1 centimetre thick on to pre-cut rounds of silicon paper.

Cook in a very slow oven overnight. Try to observe them for the first half an hour. If they colour too quickly the oven is too hot. Move them to the front with the door open until the oven cools. They are cooked when they are firm, dry and crisp with or without colour. Store the meringues in an airtight container or sealed bag.

We serve our meringues in a layered tier filled with a half cream, half pastry cream blend and various combinations of fresh berries. This dessert, more than any other we make, seems to fill people with fear that they might miss out!

Cooking in Your Oven

Pointers for (Brick Oven) Cooks

- The cook's task is to deliver food from its source to the table in a fresh, wholesome state.

- Cooking requires care and skill. Be patient with yourself as you develop these virtues.

- Avoid over-preparation, presenting food that retains its inherent qualities. Mash, puree and blend with reluctance.

- Cook with respect for yourself and your ingredients first. Approval from others is of lesser importance.

- Less is more at the table. Leave space for the next dish, the wine and tomorrow's breakfast. Don't saturate people with complexity and excess.

- The palate recognises salty, sweet, sour and bitter tastes. Flavour is tied in to our sense of smell, enabling us to enjoy a huge range of delicious experiences. Bitter is important for digestion. Hot (chilli and pepper) is experienced through the sense of touch, salt adds taste, garlic adds flavour and lemon juice adds taste and flavour. Learn to build taste and flavour as you work with understanding, balance and restraint.

- Always include fresh, watery vegetables, greens and herbs in your menu.

- Don't believe those TV cooks who say the wine you cook with must be as good as the wine you drink. (I know, you never believed them anyway!)

Cooking in Your Oven

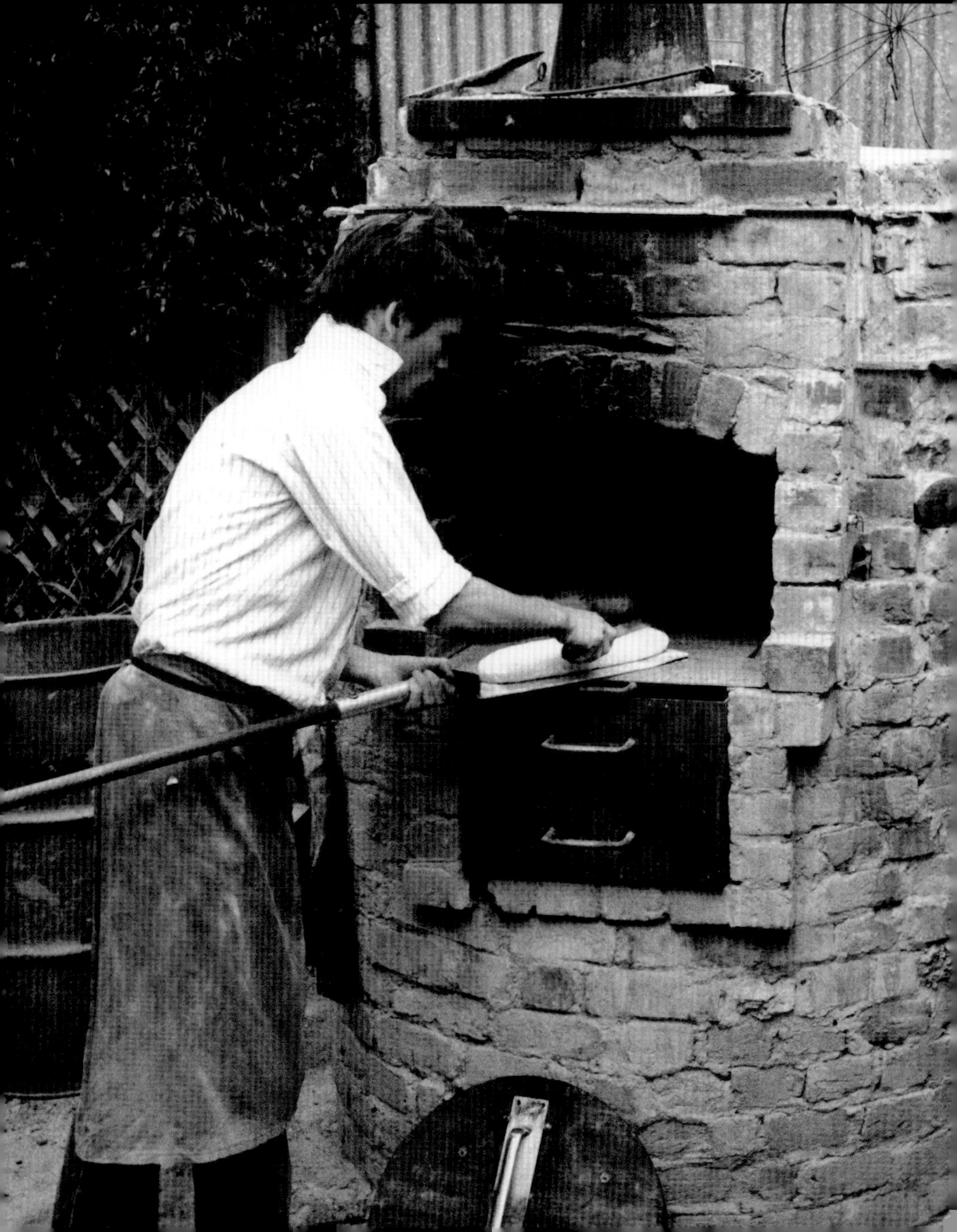

Approximate Temperature Chart for Brick Oven Cooking

450°C (hottest)	pizza
400°C	Turkish pide
400°C	vegetables and meatballs
400°C	bread
360°C	roast meat
350°C	roast vegetables
300°C	baked fish
250°C	strudel
225°C	cake
200°C	quince tart
150°C	crème caramel
125°C	blind bake pastry
100°C	almond meringue
80°C	roast almonds and seeds

Suitable thermometers are available from instrument manufacturers but you will develop a feel for the relative temperatures over time.

Metric Measuring Cup

The metric measuring cup specified in this book has a capacity of 250 ml. Clearly graduated measuring cups and jugs can therefore be used for all liquid and dry cup quantities given in the recipes. Note that:

¼ cup = 60 ml
½ cup = 125 ml
¾ cup = 185 ml
1 cup = 250 ml = ¼ litre